The Woman,
The Cat,
The Tortoise &
The Menopause

Copyright Janette Cass 2022

All rights reserved.

No part of this publication may be reproduced, stored in a retrieval system, or transmitted in any form, or by any means, electronic, mechanical, photocopying, recording or otherwise, without the prior written permission of the Publisher, except in the case of brief quotations embodied in critical reviews and certain other non-commercial uses permitted by copyright law.

For permission requests, please contact the publisher:
janette@missmenopausal.com

Illustrations by Annmarie Barnard.

Dedications

For everyone who helped, inspired
or dared me to create this little book,
and there are loads of you - a big thank you.

Especially:

Oscar & Dolly the cats.
Harry the tortoise.

Davina 'you know who'
(she'll probably never read this)
and...
all the amazing women I've met
via Miss Menopausal, who even on the
really rubbish days can still find something
to laugh about.
x

www.missmenopausal.com
facebook.com/missmenopausal

Hello!

Thank you for buying your favourite book in the whole world, even if you haven't read it yet.

Allow me to officially introduce myself; I'm the Cat...

This is me - handsome devil, eh?

Currently I'm writing this sat in the litter tray because it's the only way to get a bit of bloody peace around here.

You see, I live with 2 others...

The Woman

That's her. She's always harping on about how hot/cold/sad/bored/tired/fedup/old/itchy/confused/achey/headachey/dry/bloated/anxious/fat/dizzy/smelly/irritable (or any combination of) she is, because of something called menopause.

And him...
   the Tortoise.

He's a wise old bugger but a proper goody 2 shoes.
He just wants everyone to be happy and positive all the time. He also has a really annoying habit of reciting gushy 'inspirational' quotes that frankly make me want to puke.

Disclaimer:

While it may well be the last self-help book you ever buy, the wise words and sage advice contained within are simply based on our observations, and are merely offered as suggestions on how to think differently about midlife and menopause.

Any opinions and suggestions by Cat & Tortoise are just that: opinions & suggestions.

You are responsible for your own decisions, actions, thoughts and well, let's face it – your whole sorry state of a life, so don't blame us if you cock things up.

After all, we're just made up characters you loon!

"The helping hand you need can usually be found at the end of your own arm."

So, about this book.

The good news is you don't have to read it all at once.
Don't worry, she can't concentrate for very long these days either.

Had a shit day? Growing a better beard than your husband?

None of your clothes fit?

Fed up of waking up in a puddle of your own sweat?

Wondering what the actual fuck is happening to you?

Totally pissed off and wondering how to get your midlife back on track?

Brilliant!

You can dip in and out for a bit of straight-talking, sarcasm and honesty from my good self as often as you need.

I do like to 'keep it real'.

And if you need some kind words, occasionally this little twerp might have something useful to say too.

But I warn you...

He's so desperate for everyone to be kind to one another,

Most of the time he just talks a load of touchy-feely, flowery bollocks!

On the whole the 3 of us rub along together quite well, just trying to live our best lives. Although most days I wish the other 2 would go and live theirs elsewhere as they can be annoying shites.

"A beautiful day begins with a beautiful mindset."

" Don't you start with that annoying inspirational crap already! "

" It's when Mother Nature gives women who are knocking on a bit, a big hard hormonal kick in the fanny because puberty, periods and childbirth weren't bad enough! "

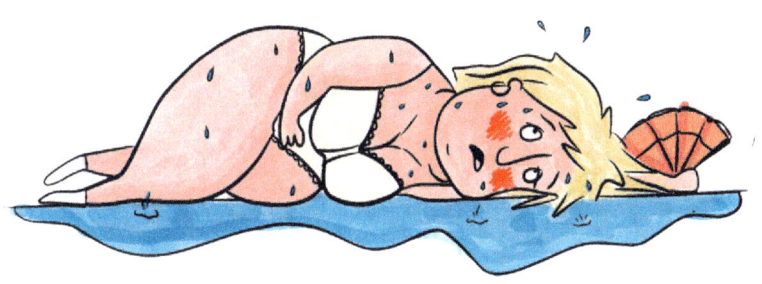

" Every day may not be good, but there's something good in every day."

" Are you going out? Good. Leave me alone - I think I've got mood poisoning! "

" I think her HRT dose might be too high as she's got hair growing where there wasn't any before."

" Where's it growing? "

" On her balls! "

" I may look like I've got no problem dealing with this menopause stuff, but if people could hear what I was really thinking I'd probably be in a mental hospital "

" And yet here you are - talking to a cat! "

" If life gives you lemons, make lemonade."

" Don't be such a dick. If life gives you lemons, you squirt someone you don't like in the eye and make yourself a very large gin and tonic. "

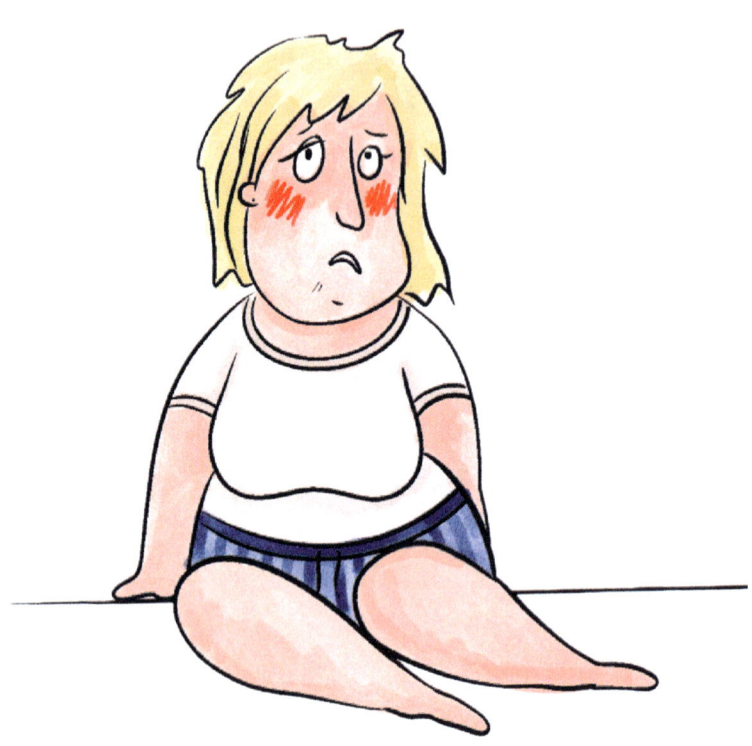

" Me too. I call this mood...

Awake! "

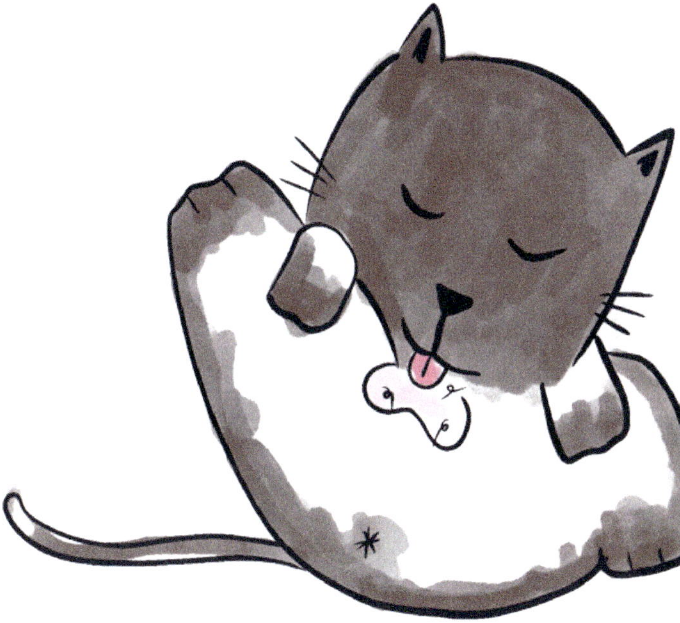

" Reach for the stars."

" Yeah, it'll stop her tits from sagging. "

" Hey Cat, why are you staring at me? "

" I'm admiring your whiskers! "

" I know that skin cells die, hair cells die, and brain cells die, but I think my fat cells must have accepted Jesus as their Saviour as those buggers seem to have eternal life. "

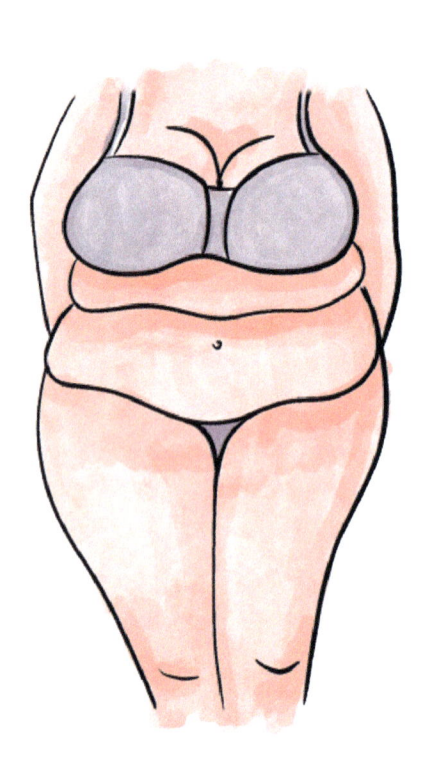

" Or... maybe it's all the cake and biscuits you eat? "

You are beautiful

You are strong

You are worth it

" Oh purrlease give it a rest. That twaddle makes me want to chuck up a furball. "

These days she was neither an early bird nor a night owl. She was more like some knackered, old pigeon.

"The quest for inner peace begins with these four words..."

Not

My

Fucking

Problem

"Life is a journey Take small steps everyday and eventually you'll get there."

"Well YOU would say that wouldn't you, short-arse?"

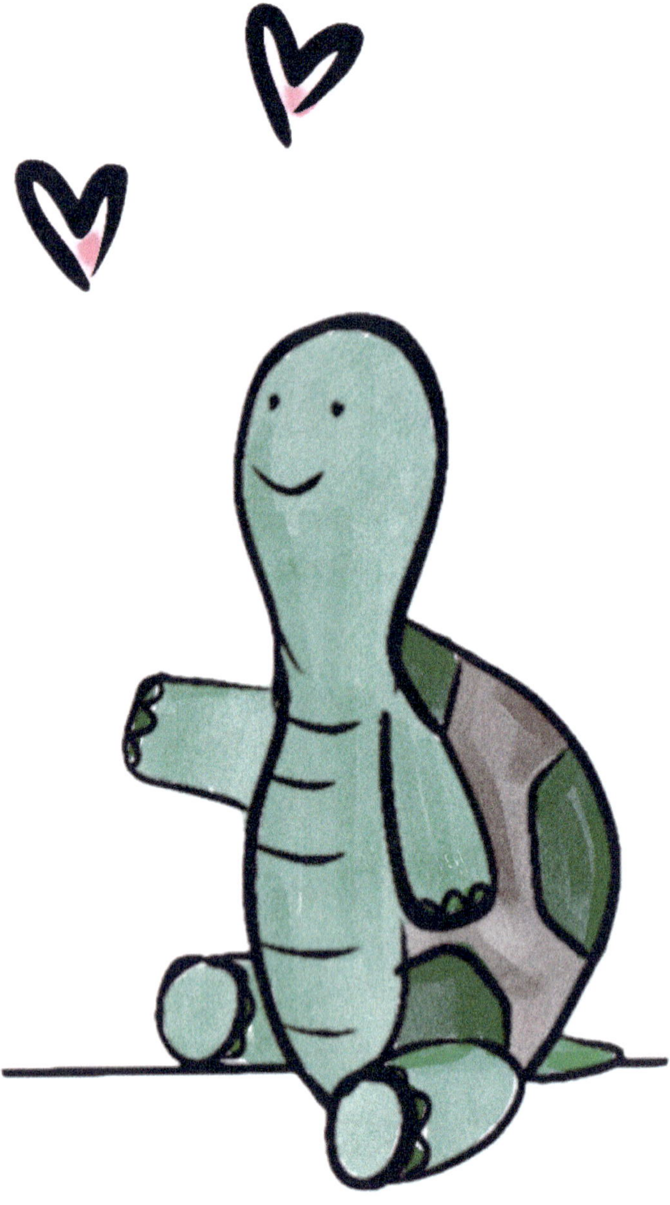

Everyone thought she'd got a trendy Spiderman tattoo but, on closer inspection, realised it was just her varicose vein playing up!

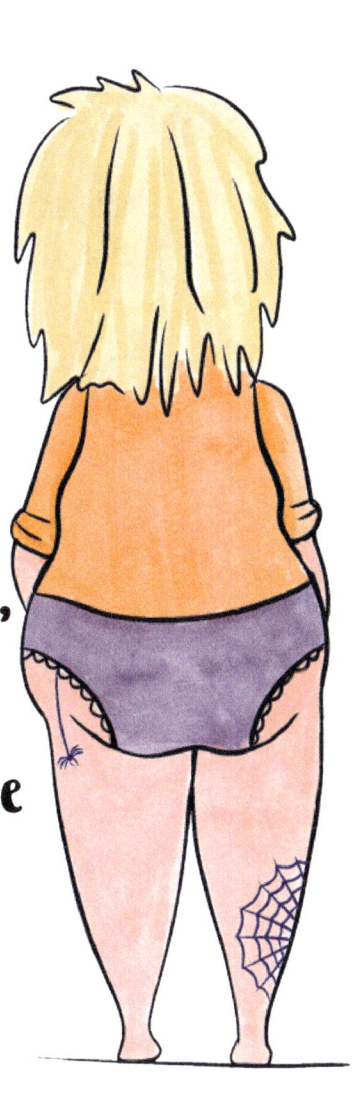

" I sometimes worry that I'm not a nice person anymore since I started having mood swings... "

" Did you:

Kill someone?

Steal from someone?

Slash their tyres?

Let Cat shit in the neighbours garden?

Erm... actually forget that one. "

"No! "

" There see. You are a good person.

Stop listening to the voices in your head telling you otherwise. "

" Oh look!
She's sneezed and pissed herself again! "

" If you want things to change,
first YOU have to change. "

" Aaaaaaargh!
Stop it -
You're making my ears
bleed. "

" Can anyone please give me some words of encouragement, so that I don't murder someone at work today? "

" There's no wine in prison! "

" I worry about her since she started this menopause. Almost every day she says she feels useless, invisible and worthless. "

" Well, tell her she needs to get a fucking grip and sort her shit out.
She only gets 1 life, not 9. "

" She wants to hear something motivational?

Tell her it's always wine o'clock somewhere! "

" It's never too late to set another goal or dream a new dream. "

" Oops, did I just roll my eyes out loud at you then? "

" Time to de-clutter. I'm going to phone the Council today and ask if it's ok for me to have a skip outside the house."

" I'm sure it'll be fine. You need all the exercise you can get, Fatty! "

" Remember, it's ok, not to be ok. "

" Tortoise, you are doing my frigging head in. "

"Dear Brian, please oh please shut down. I need to sleep."

"Who's Brian?"

"Brain, I mean brain!"

"She's always in a bad mood lately."

"Cut her some slack.

Everyone knows women over 45 are full of rage and sick of everyone else's bullshit!"

" Hello. I'm just in the middle of the menopause. Can I call you back in about 5 years? "

"What ARE you doing?"

"It's one of those celebrity menopause candles. I'm sniffing Gwyneth's fanny...

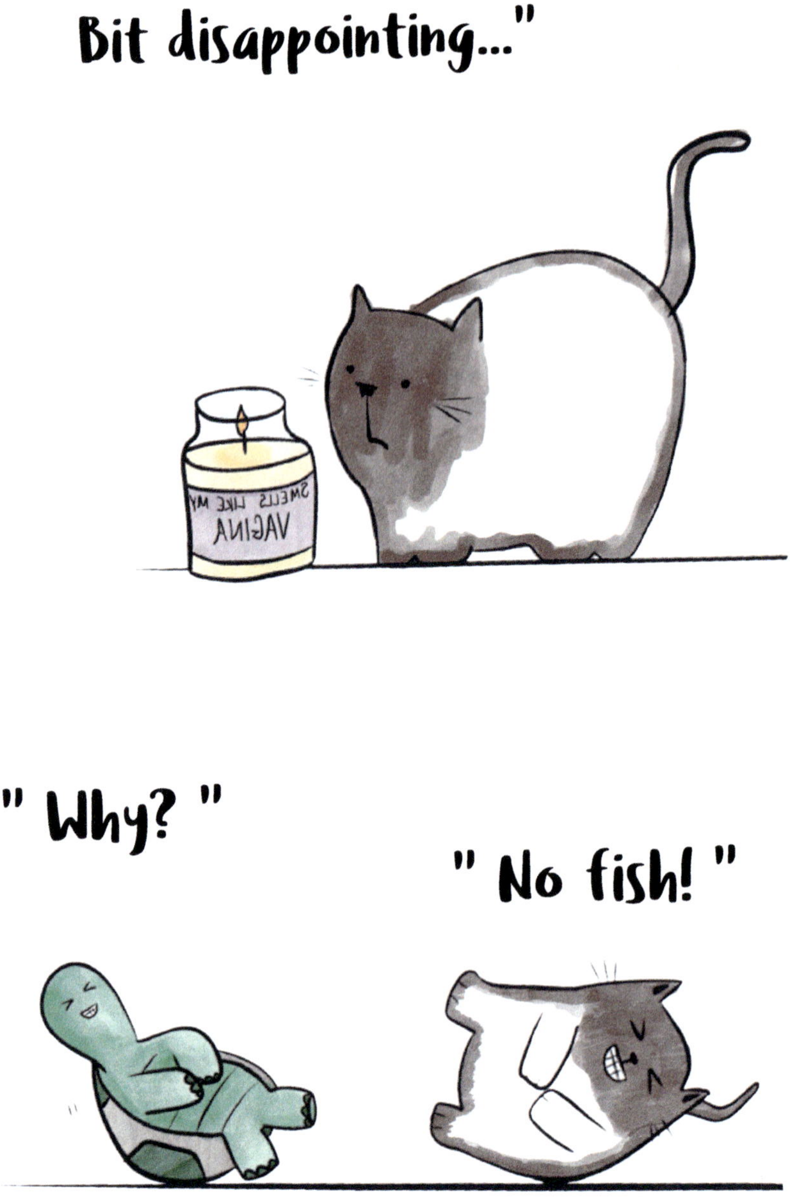
Bit disappointing..."
SMELLS LIKE MY VAGINA
" Why? "
" No fish! "

" If it sounds like fun and you want to do it; do it.
Pleasing others is not as important as pleasing yourself."

"Hurray, you little twerp! That's the first thing you've said that's made any sense!"

Forget growing old gracefully,

What she really needed was a moisturiser to hide the fact she'd been tired since 2008.

" Mama just hit menopause, no more children can be bred, because her ovaries are dead."

" Ssssshhhhh....

She's having a nap – she said no-one is to disturb her. "

" Too bloody late for that, she's disturbed enough already! "

" Yesterday is history, tomorrow a mystery and today is a gift.
That's why we call it the present."

" How about I present you with a punch on the nose you annoying little turdnugget? "

" She had some of her
menopausal mates
round today,
The hot flushes were so bad
they steam cleaned
the carpets! "

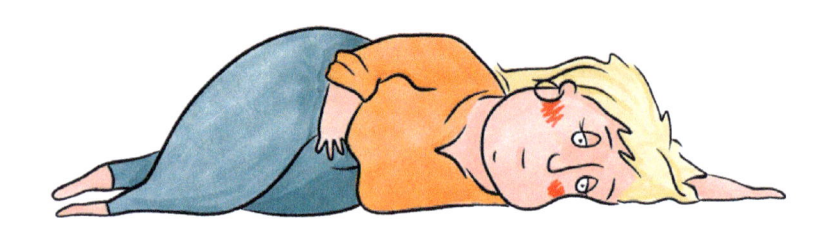

" I'm a person who wants to do a lot of things, trapped in the body of a person who just wants to sleep. "

" Me too! "

" I'm not waiting for the stars
to align -
just my hormones... "

" Forget Meno-Pause.

I wish someone would just invent a Meno-Stop button and spare us ALL the aggro."

" Live every day like it's your last. "

" If you don't shut your gob this may well be your last day! "

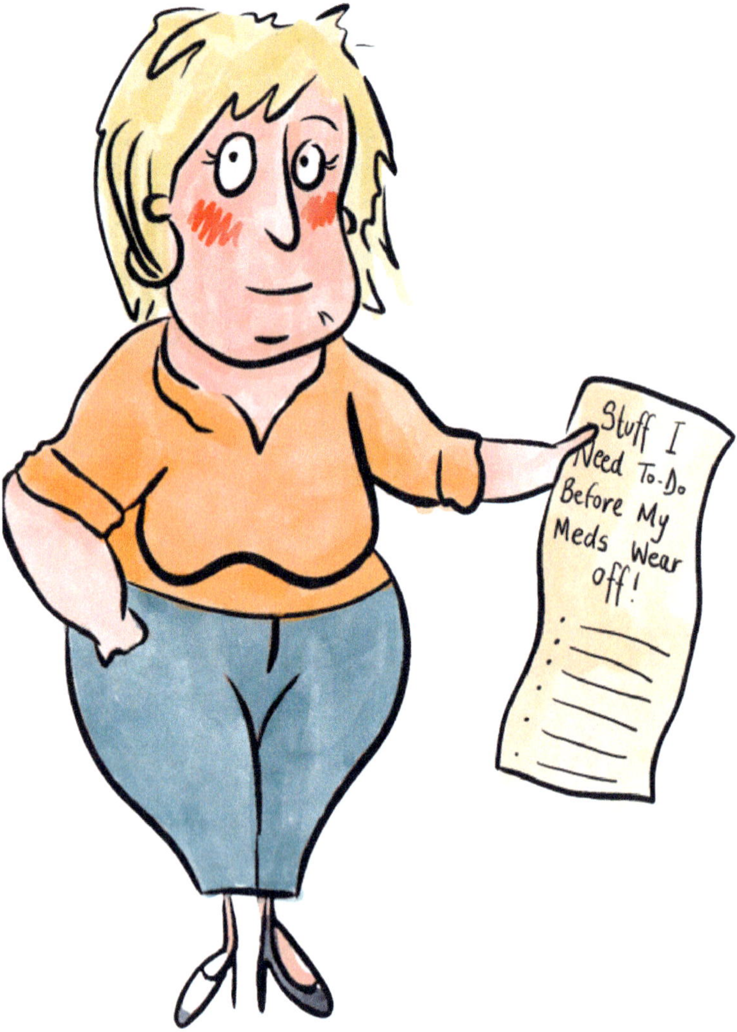
Stuff I Need To-Do Before My Meds Wear off!

" Here we fucking go again.
I mean...
Good Morning! "

"Morning Cat. Did you sleep well?"

" No I didnt.

Her restless legs were in and out of the duvet so many times I feel like we've danced the hokey cokey all night "

"They say wearing a magnet in your knickers helps with hot flushes...

but my arse keeps getting stuck to the fridge door!"

" She believed she could, so she did. "

" I believe I should show you my middle finger. So I will! "

" I'm going to treat myself
to a new hairdo.
I wonder what cut will make
me look younger? "

" How about a power cut? "

I am Wonder Woman!

I wonder why I went upstairs?

I wonder where my keys are?

I wonder who will annoy me today?

I wonder where my waistline went?

I wonder if I will ever regain my sanity?

"If you're happy and you know it, it's your meds."

" I'm exhausted from always pretending to be stronger than I really feel..."

" Some things matter a lot, but a lot of things really don't matter much at all.

So stop worrying about stupid shit that is out of your control.

Bugger me, I sounded like Tortoise then.

Shoot me now! "

"When did the menopause become the moanapause?"

"I think that Davina woman is to blame."

" A good man can make you feel sexy, strong and able to take on the world. "

" Oh sorry, thats Gin...

Gin does that. "

" If you see someone without
a smile,
give them
one of yours. "

"Can you see the 'fuck you' in my smile?"

" I miss the days when I could get out of bed without making sound effects. "

" Her husband thinks she is a sex object."

"Why?"

"Because every time he asks for sex,
she objects!"

" There's nothing like taking your bra off at the end of a tough day. "

"It must be a magic bra because, when you took it off, all the wrinkles disappeared from your face! "

" It's important to have a twinkle in your wrinkle. "

" Well you would say that, you're a tortoise and full of wrinkles you total moron. "

" How did it happen? One minute I was young and carefree, the next I'm excited because the grocery delivery has no missing items or substitutions! "

"Whoopy doo!
I'm totally underwhelmed
for you,

Now where's my dinner?"

" I don't think I'm good enough to do anything much with my life at my age,

I suppose I should just be grateful for what I've got? "

" F.F.S - Another day, another whinge.

Wake up and smell the coffee.

Sometimes you've just got to pull your big pants up and tell your own bullshit to shove off. "

" Always try to be the best version of yourself. "

" Hmmm... I assume you didn't hear her shouting "WANKER" at the parcel delivery man earlier? "

" Wouldn't it be nice if they put little gifts & messages inside packs of sanitary towels?"

"Saying what?

Sorry you feel like your uterus is falling out - here's a bar of chocolate you moody cow?"

" These days I can't tell if
I do actually have some
free time,
or if I'm just forgetting
everything. "

" Positive thinking is all well and good, but I find a 'Zero fucks given' really helps me to rise and shine. "

" In a world where you can
be anything,
be kind. "

" Okay, here goes... "

I'm sorry for all the mean, shitty, awful, accurate things I ever said about you.

Now do one, dickhead! "

" Bloody hell, you're actually laughing. What's happened? "

" I accidently took the wrong medication this morning.
The good news is I'm protected from fleas and worms for the next 3 months! "

" You are enough. "

" I've just about had enough of you and these gushy cliches, you little tosser. "

And just like that...

Fed up of listening to Tortoise talk out of his arse and the Woman drone on day after day about her menopause, Cat decided he was not cut out to be an emotional support pet after all.

"Bugger this,
I'm off!"

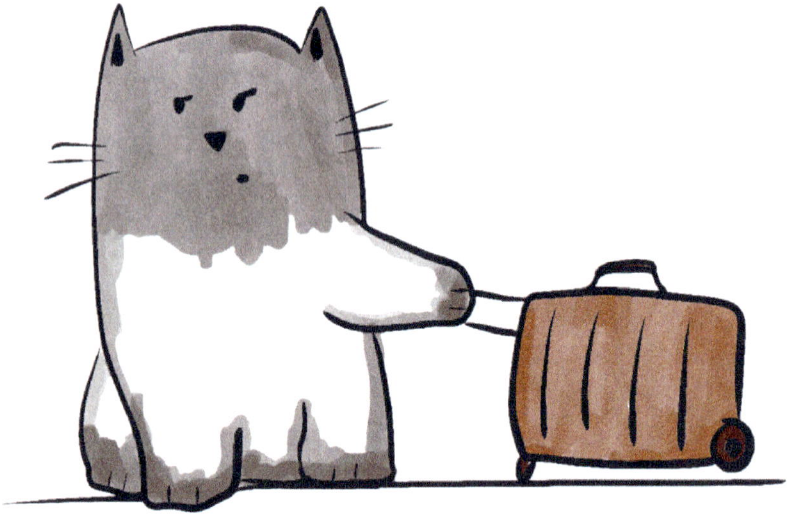

" Please don't go.
You're my best friend! "

" And I suppose you're mine too, but sometimes you're such a patronising little nob. "

" Remember.
This is just one chapter,
not your whole life story.
You still get to decide what
happens next. "

" Oh FFS, pack it in will you ?
I know she's got
brain fog but
look, even she's
got the
message now. "

Being Menopausal

I've sweaty boobs, and a roll of back fat,
itchy flaps too, but best not talk
about that.

Leaking lady bits, and a bristly chin,
distant memories of the days I was thin.

I'm drying up, both inside and out,
with my fluffy big toes and
my wiry-haired snout.

Big knickers I pull up nice and high,
my knockers now heading South,
towards my thigh.

I can't even sneeze without
doing a piddle,
and I've 2 rolls of fat stored
around my middle.

These days I'm always hot,
except in the buff,
I hardly sleep, but I'm made of
tough stuff.

I may suffer often from bad excess gas,
but you, menopause symptoms,
can go kiss my ass.

With tweezers at hand for the
hairs on my chin,
this menopause is a battle,
I'm determined to win.

A big jar of anti-wrinkle cream
will do its best,
But good friends and laughter
can help sort the rest.

So, I'm going to tackle all of this,
with a smile on my face,

And of course keep a
panty liner firmly in place!

THE END

Here's a few blank pages so you can write down your bucket list, or all the stuff you know you're never going to be arsed to do, but it'll look good when someone else picks up this book!

Printed in Great Britain
by Amazon